Ceciel de Bie

The J. Paul Getty Museum, Los Angeles

My Brother
Vincent van Gogh

Words of gratitude

I would like to take this opportunity to thank all the
people who have worked with me and have made the
book My Brother Vincent van Gogh possible. In particular
I would like to mention Reinoud Leenen and Sjraar van
Heugten, who have been a great help with the text.
I am very grateful to Cees de Jong for his deep-rooted
faith in this book.

Dutch edition © 2002 V+K Publishing, Blaricum, The Netherlands
Ceciel de Bie, Amsterdam

First published in the United States of America in 2002 by
Getty Publications
1200 Getty Center Drive, Suite 500
Los Angeles, California 90049-1682
www.getty.edu

Christopher Hudson, Publisher
Mark Greenberg, Editor in Chief

Colophon
Concept, text and illustrations Ceciel de Bie, Amsterdam
Consultant Sjraar van Heugten, Amsterdam
Translation Kate Wiliams, Leiden
Graphic design Corine Teuben V+K Design, Blaricum
Ceciel de Bie, Amsterdam
Cover illustration Majel, Amsterdam
Lithography and printing Snoeck-Ducaju & Zoon, Ghent

Library of Congress Control Number 2002107597

ISBN 0-89236-711-3

What can be found in this book

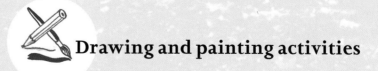
Drawing and painting activities

All about our childhood dreams

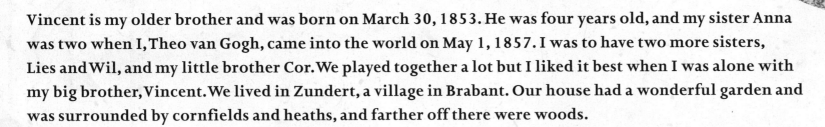

Vincent is my older brother and was born on March 30, 1853. He was four years old, and my sister Anna was two when I, Theo van Gogh, came into the world on May 1, 1857. I was to have two more sisters, Lies and Wil, and my little brother Cor. We played together a lot but I liked it best when I was alone with my big brother, Vincent. We lived in Zundert, a village in Brabant. Our house had a wonderful garden and was surrounded by cornfields and heaths, and farther off there were woods.

There was always something going on at one of the farms. We would scramble up the haystacks, and sometimes we were allowed to help the farmer. Or we would build sandcastles, with deep moats around them. Vincent's turrets were always higher; he was extremely good at everything. Everyone could see that we were brothers because we both had pale-blue eyes and reddish-blond hair.

In the autumn we roamed through the woods. We filled our baskets with chestnuts, acorns, leaves, and stones and sometimes found the skeleton of a small animal. It was often difficult to guess what the animal might be because there were always a few bones missing. In the summer we would set off with my father to spot the lark. We peered up into the sky endlessly, until we got cricks in the neck, trying to see a tiny dot moving about up there.

At home we collected prints

Vincent and I were always together until he had to go to school. It was a village school where lots of farmers' sons went. My father thought it was making Vincent far too rough, so they sent him to a boarding school. I missed him, and playing outside wasn't as much fun without him.

I only saw Vincent during the holidays. I was given lessons at home by a schoolteacher. When I was fourteen we moved, and I had to walk six kilometers to school then.

I have very fond memories of family visits to my uncle, who was also called Vincent, but everyone called him Cent. He and my aunt didn't have any children so they spoiled us terribly.

Portraits of Theo and Vincent
as boys in Brabant

Uncle Cent was an art dealer, and that was only too obvious when you went to his house. His country house had a gallery built onto it, and the most marvelous paintings were hanging everywhere. It was the first time that Vincent and I had ever seen real paintings. Some were painted very beautifully; there was so much to be seen. At home we collected prints. This included pictures of paintings, but they were always in black and white. My brother was the more fanatical, sticking the prints into a large scrapbook.

When Vincent finished school, he had to go to work. My Uncle Cent needed someone good for his art dealer's shop in The Hague. Vincent moved to The Hague to work at our uncle's art business. He enjoyed the work. My parents boasted about him all the time, about how hard-working he was and how good he was at it. I missed him terribly. When I was fifteen, I was allowed to go and stay with him for a few days. I was overjoyed; we had a really good time. One day when we were out walking, we got caught in a tremendous downpour but we managed to find shelter near a windmill until the rain stopped. We drank a large mug of milk while we were there, and we carried on chatting; we had such a lot of news to catch up on. Vincent wanted to show me everything, so those few days just flew by.

5

We wrote letters to one another

When I got home, I realized that I hadn't been able to tell him everything, not by a long shot. So that is why we started writing letters to one another. I couldn't possibly have known then that we would do so for the rest of our lives. I was sixteen years old, and just like Vincent I went to work as an art dealer in Uncle Hein's business. It meant that I had to move to Brussels. My father took me there, but when he went away, I felt so abandoned and lonely. The hustle and bustle of that city was quite a change from the village I came from. Fortunately I had a lot of work to do, packing and unpacking paintings and doing all sorts of odd jobs. For the first time, I saw paintings by artists whom I previously had only known by name. If a new painting was delivered I always wanted to be there, just out of curiosity. I wrote about them to Vincent because he knew so much more about them than I did. I was interested to hear which painters he thought were good and why that

Send a card showing your own collection

You will need scissors, glue, cardboard, drawing or painting materials, colored paper, and old newspapers or pictures.
Vincent and Theo were always collecting things. First, all kinds of things from the woods, then beautiful prints, and later on even paintings.
Do you have a collection of your own? It may be anything, for example a few shells or pebbles. Cut the cardboard into rectangular shapes, the size of picture postcards. Choose the most beautiful objects from your collection. Then use them as models for a work of art to be made on the card. Use a variety of materials. You can send the card to someone in your family or to a good friend. In this way you can tell them your latest news and show them what you collect at the same time.

was. Vincent wanted me to start concentrating more on collecting artists' prints, which is how our joint art collection started off. Later we added real paintings to the collection, too.

Vincent in London

Vincent moved to London. For a while his work went very well, and he earned enough money to send some of it home. He visited museums to admire the English painters, and he sent us the nicest drawings. But after a while he became miserable. My brother didn't feel at home anymore in the world of art dealers.

At Christmas the whole family sat around the dining table at long last. I was so happy to see Vincent again. He told me about his plans to teach at a private school in England. He couldn't manage at work anymore. He wanted to mean something to other people. Fortunately he still loved paintings, which is what we talked about most of the time. It was difficult to say goodbye. I soon received a letter in which he told me about his new place of work. From the school you had a view of the sea, and on his first day he went for a long walk along the shore with his pupils. He had even included a piece of seaweed in the letter.

Goupil's art gallery, The Hague

Vincent wanted to do something good

Vincent wrote me more and more about God and the Bible. He went so far as to say that he had plans to become a minister, just like our father and grandfather. I found it hard to imagine. Vincent as a minister? But he really wanted to tell people about God, and he wanted to do something good to help people too. He was planning to study theology. In the end the studying didn't go well at all. Nevertheless he persevered. My brother isn't one to give up easily.

Vincent went to Belgium to work as a minister in Borinage, a mine workers' district where lots of poor people were living. He visited the sick, taught the children, read out loud from the Bible, and began to draw more and more often. The churchgoers didn't want my brother to work for them any longer. They thought he was strange and couldn't understand him at all. The fact that he lived with a poor family of mine workers and gave away all his belongings was totally unacceptable in their eyes.

Vincent becomes an artist

Jean-François Millet

August, 1880

Vincent has decided to become an artist. How relieved I am that he is to stop working for the mine workers. That heavy work isn't good for him, and he takes everything far too much to heart. Just recently, drawing has given him so much pleasure. He has been writing to me about it more and more often in his letters. I told him that I believed that he would be a painter one day. I think I spotted this even earlier than Vincent did. 'Me an artist? That is not the sort of job for me, is it?' he had asked, amazed. Vincent wouldn't hear another word on the subject. But now he is even going to move to Brussels so that he can take drawing lessons and meet other artists.

Vincent is living with my parents again

Etten in Brabant April-December 1881

I am going to send Vincent money on a regular basis, I earn enough, and I think it is important that my brother should be able to carry on with his art. He sends me drawings of farmers working on the land. They are digging, sowing, or mowing, and he tries to copy all the different poses in his drawings. He thinks it's a shame that they have to do such hard work and that they are so poor. I think Vincent's drawings are still very wooden. I wonder whether they will ever amount to anything. He himself thinks that he must be able to draw really well if he is ever to become a good painter.

I am finding little drawings more regularly in Vincent's letters. He calls them his 'thumbnail sketches.' Vincent doesn't just copy prints but goes outside a lot too. He asks the farmers if they will pose for him in working positions. If you give them some money they usually will. This has led him to draw quite a lot of diggers, sowers, plowmen, and farmers' wives.

8

Vincent's great master, Millet

Vincent's shining example is the French countryside painter Jean-François Millet (1814–1875).

He writes to me that you learn to look best through the drawings and paintings of Millet, who draws and paints farmers and farmers' wives at work. He often paints the landscape accompanying them, too. He wants to show as authentically as possible how hard farm life is. This is the subject Vincent is crazy about. Millet thinks that as an artist you should live in the countryside like a farmer, and he is proud of coming from a farming family.

Many prints have been made of his paintings and drawings. Vincent and I have a whole collection now. Sometimes we cut prints out of magazines. Vincent uses them as examples to copy from in order to get some practice. In the art trade I sometimes see paintings of Millet's. They are superb.

The farmer's wife is stirring a large pitcher of milk in order to make butter.

Woman Churning Butter, Etten, 1881. Drawing, crayon, and watercolor

Jean-François Millet, Woman Churning Butter, 1855-56. Drawing

In the painting we can see a farmer; he is utterly exhausted. He is using his hoe to lean on so he can have a little rest. We can see stones in the soil. Removing them is hard work. Millet has paid a great deal of attention to the landscape. He has even painted the tiniest plants and blades of grass.

Jean-François Millet, Man with a Hoe, 1860-62. Oil on canvas

Farmer Leaning on a Spade, 1881. Drawing, pastel, and watercolor

My brother is not himself anymore. He writes the craziest of things, for instance, that he wants to be as happy as a lark in the spring. He is head-over-heels in love with our sweet cousin Kee whose husband died very recently.

He does all kinds of things so that she will realize how much he loves her. He writes her the kindest letters, but Kee is not in love with Vincent, and it took ages before he would actually believe it.

10

This drawing was made in our parent's garden. The outline was done in pencil, and after that, Vincent worked further in pen and ink. When Vincent was given a box of paints by Uncle Cent, he started giving some of his drawings a little color.

The Rectory Garden with Lean-To, 1881. Drawing, ink, pastel, and pencil

Carpenter's Shed and Yard,
1882. Drawing, pencil, ink,
and watercolor

Vincent's Studio in The Hague

Vincent has had an argument with my father and mother.
They think that Vincent should leave our cousin Kee in
peace. I think it is awful for my parents, and I don't
understand Vincent. They mean well. Perhaps it's all for
the good that he no longer lives at my father and mother's
and has now gone to The Hague.

There is enough to draw, he writes. His studio window
looks out on a carpenter's shed. The people who work
there are always busy. There are a lot of workshops in the

town, and the beach and sand dunes are not far away. He loves to just roam around.

Vincent wants to see me again soon. He is curious to hear what I think about his work. I would very much like to see him, but I can't leave the business just like that.

Vincent writes about his new girlfriend. She is called Sien, and she was already pregnant before Vincent met her. She is always willing to pose, and she shows endless patience with Vincent. It is very nice for Vincent because it is difficult to get models. Sometimes they promise to go to the studio but then don't show up. Sien and her daughter have moved in with Vincent. They have absolutely nothing, and he is keen to help them.

I have written to Vincent that I understand how nice it must be to no longer be on his own, but I can't afford to support a whole family. I hope he understands.

Endless walks

My brother has moved to Drenthe without Sien and her children. He finds having to leave them behind difficult, particularly the little boy because he is very fond of him. Lots of painters go to Drenthe because it is so beautiful there.

Vincent wrote to me about fields covered in pink heather and the flocks of sheep roaming around and old houses with moss roofs. He has been walking for miles and miles from village to village. The views over the fields are highly panoramic; the people and horses seem so small they are like tiny dots.

Vincent writes that it is cold where he is and it rains a lot. I hope he has taken a warm coat with him. He lives in a tiny attic without much light. Some people sneer at his work because they don't understand what he's doing.

Vincent often has to wait quite awhile for my letters and money. And it is difficult to buy painting materials. He always wants to be painting.

Vincent thinks that I, too, should become a painter. I like art a lot, but that is very different from doing your own paintings. I can't just leave my job. How would we earn a living if I did?

I hope that Vincent isn't feeling too lonely. I am going to write to him straightaway.

Do a drawing out in the countryside

You will need a sketchbook, a pencil, and colored pencils. When he was outdoors Vincent always had a sketchbook with him. This meant he could always do a drawing. If you are going walking in the park or in the countryside then take your drawing materials with you. If you find a nice place or see something special then you can always draw it. First, sketch it using fine lines. What do you think is important in your drawing? Give that more emphasis. The trees in the distance can be seen less clearly than the plants closer by; try to show that in your drawing.

Vincent is continuing to send his work

Nuenen 1883-November 1885

I think that Vincent felt too lonely in Drenthe because he has suddenly moved back to my parents.' My father is now the minister in Nuenen. Vincent writes that he has fitted out the washhouse at the back of the family home as a studio. He tells me that our parents think of him as a shaggy dog who bounces into the room with muddy paws and gets under everyone's feet.

He thinks I am not doing enough to sell his work. It would do Vincent good to know that I just recently wrote a letter to our sister Wil in which I said that I thought that Vincent would become a great artist. Fortunately he is continuing to send work. He has asked me if I would consider the money I pay him as payment for the drawings and paintings which I receive from him.

My brother enjoys being with the weavers in Nuenen. They work at home, and when they have woven a piece of cloth they try to sell it to the textile factory. They make all kinds of things there. Their work is a hard slog, and they earn very little for their efforts. In his attempts to draw the loom as accurately as possible, Vincent has studied it time and time again. You can see the loom quite well against the bare light-colored wall.

Vincent is sending me this drawing with still more drawings of the weavers. He thinks his little weavers have turned out well and hopes that I can sell them. I think Vincent's drawings are getting better all the time. But it's such a shame that he hardly uses any color. He thinks he should first be able to draw well before starting to use color.

Colors weavers use

Vincent often talks about the colors the weavers use. He wants to paint with streaks of paint like their threads and then start weaving with the different colors. The pieces look gray, but if you look close up, you can see red, blue, yellow, black, and white threads. With all those different colors, the materials are never dull.

Experimenting with drawing materials

You will need thick drawing paper, hard and soft drawing pencils, a brush, a drawing pen, an oil crayon, pastel crayons, ink, and white paint.

Do a drawing of somebody in action. For example, your mother gardening, your father doing some woodwork, or one of your friends playing ball. Get all your drawing materials together. You can use white paint to put accents in your drawing. Vincent used white paint in his drawing of the carpenter's shed. He was always experimenting with his materials. What happens if you rub out soft crayon? What's the difference if you press hard or gently when drawing in pencil? What happens if you dilute ink with water? Or if you draw onto wet paint? You can try out lots of other ways too. Use what you discover in your drawings.

Weaver, 1884. Drawing, pencil,
pen and ink, and watercolor

His first masterpiece

April 1885

Vincent is very interested in how light works. In the evenings he paints or draws the farmers at home around their tables, which are lit by oil lamps. During the day he draws them by daylight, often near the window. The houses are dark inside. If the light falls through a small window, you can see backlight. Looking from the dark into the light: that is what Vincent is interested in. With all the different sorts of light, the world is constantly changing.

I have asked Vincent to send his best painting. He has done a lot of studies for farmers' portraits, but I have not seen a large painting from him yet. He started on his first masterpiece at once.

What is your favorite food?

You will need thick paper, paint, and brushes.
Vincent painted The Potato Eaters. *Would you like to eat potatoes,*
and only potatoes, every day? What do you like eating most of all?
Could it be chocolate? If it is, do a painting of The Chocolate Eaters.

Vincent painted *The Potato Eaters* from memory. Before he did it he often went to see a farming family he was friendly with. He first made sketches of all the members of the family in the room with their belongings. An oil lamp is lighting the tabletop. The farmers and farmers' wives are pricking their forks into the steaming potatoes on their plates. They are tired from working hard on the land, and they don't say very much to one another. A woman is

16

The Potato Eaters, 1885.
Oil on canvas

pouring the coffee, but Vincent has made that up because they never drink coffee with their evening meal.

In the painting Vincent shows that he is good at painting chiaroscuro (light-dark). In Vincent's view you should make things dark by using colors too, so he has used red, blue, and yellow paint to do so. It is difficult to find all those colors in the dark painting. Could he have thought of 'his little weavers' woolen cloth when he was painting it?

Vincent ought to see the Impressionists' paintings some time! The Impressionists use such fresh, pale colors. Their paintings are very light compared with Vincent's *Potato Eaters*. I think the painting is old-fashioned, but I don't dare tell Vincent, particularly because he is so pleased with it himself.

17

Among the artists in Paris

March 1886

At work a letter is pushed into my hand. It is from Vincent. He writes that he will wait for me in the Louvre Museum. I am surprised because I had asked Vincent not to come to Paris yet. I first want to rent a larger house. My apartment is so small, there is no room for a studio in it. Despite the shock, I am still very happy he is here.

We went to see the paintings in the Louvre straightaway. We stood in front of a painting by Rembrandt for quite awhile. Vincent is always enthusiastic about how well Rembrandt can paint chiaroscuro. And he was telling me about the unusual color combinations that the painter Eugène Delacroix uses. I said, 'Vincent, wait until you see the paintings by the Impressionists. You won't know what's hit you. They use such bright colors, straight out of the tube. The Impressionists want to paint the light. They are mad about the light because it is always changing. This is why they think that you can't really paint the things you see around you at all. You can only give an impression of what you can see.'

We went for a walk that afternoon in the district where I live. It is a bit messy and there are allotments nearby, and even windmills. Vincent likes these little streets with tiny shops and all the different types of people walking about there. He feels more at ease among them than with respectable middle-class people who veil themselves in clouds of perfume. We went to Moulin de la Galette for a cup of coffee. During the day it is a bar, and in the evenings people dance there. 'Perhaps I will meet someone I know,' I thought, 'because I would so like to introduce my brother to people.'

That evening we changed the apartment around together so that Vincent was able to find enough space for his easel and paints after all.

The Eiffel Tower was built for the world exhibition in Paris, 1889.

Opposite: Photo-collage of Paris

Experiments with color and paint

Vincent has started taking lessons at Fernand Cormon's studio. He wants to learn to draw better and hopes to be given tips. He had heard that Cormon is a good teacher and not too strict either. They use live models or plaster statues for their drawings.

Vincent talks nineteen to the dozen about Henri de Toulouse-Lautrec and Émile Bernard and other artists. It seems as if Vincent thinks meeting them is more important than the lessons. There he can see that all those young painters are doing quite different things from him.

Self-portrait

We have moved to a larger apartment on the third floor of a house on the Rue Lepic. Vincent is working very hard now. I think he likes painting self-portraits because then he can experiment in peace with color and various colored streaks of paint. Sometimes he stays in his studio for hours on end. I don't even dare to take him a cup of coffee because I am much too scared I will disturb him.

In Paris, Vincent has painted almost thirty self-portraits.

Atelier Cormon, 1885

Self-portrait Wearing a Gray Felt Hat, 1888. Oil on canvas

This self-portrait has a radiant corona (circle) around the face done in streaks of blue-colored paint. All the streaks of paint can easily be seen. You don't see a gray hat like that very often. It is typical of my brother. It makes him look artistic.

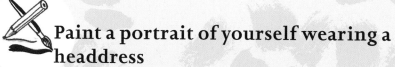 ## Paint a portrait of yourself wearing a headdress

You will need a mirror, drawing paper, paint, and brushes. *Vincent was in high spirits which is why he put on a beautiful gray hat. Paint a portrait of yourself with some sort of headdress. Look into the mirror. How are you feeling today, are you happy or sad or something in between? Choose a headdress to show your mood. It might be anything for example a jester's cap, an American Indian headdress or a wig. Paint it in dots and streaks. Your self-portrait will show what mood you are in.*

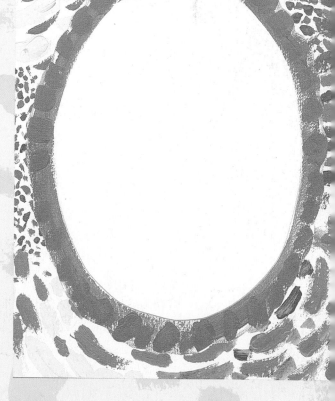

Vincent paints in dots and streaks. The colors in the background – the green and the red – vibrate.

Bridges over the Seine near Asnières, 1887. Oil on canvas

I regretted that thought at once

The paintings in Vincent's studio are stacked crisscross all over the place, there is messy paint everywhere, and the house could do with a good cleaning. That's not all; it's becoming more and more difficult to live with my brother under one roof. One minute Vincent is friendly and saying nice things to me, and the next he is really unbearable!

Through Vincent I have met a great number of artists; he makes friends very easily. He is curious to see what they are doing and wants to see everything. Because of his new surroundings Vincent has started using much lighter and brighter colors. He is also selecting different subjects to paint, like the River Seine, parks, factory yards, and places on the outskirts of the city. He is out on the town a lot with his friend Émile Bernard, who has a studio in Asnières, in his father's garden. They paint together and get on with one another very well.

In the early days we had lots of visitors. Vincent brought his artist friends home with him. But after awhile it quieted down. My friends don't come very often because Vincent can be so sharp with people during conversations. He always wants to convince everyone of his own ideas. If it leads to arguments I don't know what to do to calm Vincent down. When I get home from a hard day's work, I don't always feel like a discussion on art. My brother can't stop his train of thought, as so much goes on in that head of his.

One night I couldn't sleep. I thought: 'I can't stand this much longer. Vincent will have to look for a house of his own,' but I regretted thinking that straightaway. Of course I don't want Vincent to go, however difficult he is at times. He is my brother, and I can't abandon him, not ever. Vincent wants to help me too. He is trying to exchange his paintings for works by his artist friends, so that he can make my art collection larger. He hopes I might be able to start my own business. Vincent knows that having my own business is my dream. It is difficult working for a boss. If I want to buy paintings from young unknown artists I can't always get permission. Fortunately I am now allowed to hang paintings by less well-known artists on one floor of the shop.

Vincent with Bernard on the Bank of the Seine, 1886

A staircase strewn with petals

When I walked up the stairs I saw that the steps were strewn with yellow, red, blue, pink, and white petals. Has Vincent been given flowers again? People he knows send him bouquets every week. Vincent often paints flowers. He tries to get the colors as intense and bright as possible. He is using combinations involving red and green, purple with yellow, and blue with orange more often now. This makes everything look more glaring. The colors 'explode' more, and that is the main idea too. He wants to exchange his flower paintings for works by other artists. Or might he be able to sell his still lifes of flowers?

How does a fresh flower turn into a wilted flower?

You will need four sheets of drawing paper and colored pencils or paint and brushes.

Vincent painted fresh and shriveled up flowers. Pick or buy a brightly colored flower or bunch of flowers. Paint or draw your flower or bunch of flowers every three days. Don't forget to write down the day. Can you see what happens to the colors and to the shapes of the flowers as time passes by? After twelve days have passed you will have done four paintings or drawings. Stick these together in the correct order. You have then made a comic-strip of the life of the flower.

Fresh sunflowers

My brother always brings home sunflowers from the flower stall on the corner. 'I've got some more!' he shouts happily as he comes rushing in. As soon as the flowers have been put into a vase, he immediately starts to paint them in ever more vivid colors.

Bowl with Sunflowers, Roses, and Other Flowers, 1886. Oil on canvas

Two Cut Sunflowers, 1887.
Oil on canvas

Vincent has exchanged this painting for one of Paul Gauguin's, one that used to hang above Gauguin's bed.

Dried sunflowers

I am never allowed to throw away the sunflowers that have finished flowering; the whole lot has to be dried. Vincent thinks the structure of their hearts is so lovely. He paints the hundreds of sunflower seeds. Dried flowers are always a little brown. He paints the background with a lot of streaks of colored paint. I had seen that a red lacquered Chinese box had been lying in Vincent's studio for quite some time. I only found out what was in it when Émile came round one afternoon. Vincent showed us the balls of wool in it with great care. 'Look,' he said. 'I use these balls before I start painting. I can make all kinds of color combinations with the woolen threads to see if they will be any good in my paintings. This saves me wasting expensive oil paints. I keep some balls because I think the combination is so beautiful that I may be able to use them for another painting. My Chinese box is my color support-system.'

25

Vincent's artist friends

Vincent has gotten to know lots of artists: Camille Pissarro and his oldest son, Lucien; Georges Seurat; Paul Signac; Louis Anquetin; and Paul Gauguin. They all want to be in Paris, the world capital of art, which is where it is all happening. They think that painting should be done differently. If you want to record something you can do that with a photograph. Painting a subject as an exact copy is old-fashioned. They think that you should be allowed to choose your own colors.

It is contagious because Vincent is beginning to experiment in his work, too. He is doing it his own way. His paintings never look like the work of other artists. He's a live wire, that brother of mine, because, apart from painting, he also organizes exhibitions of his friends' work in bars and restaurants. I want to show as many of their paintings as possible at the art dealer's where I work.

Henri de Toulouse-Lautrec's studio in Montmartre is a meeting place for young painters. Vincent likes to go there.

Lucien Pissarro, Drawing of
Vincent Talking, 1887

Henri de Toulouse-Lautrec
in his Studio

They draw quite a few portraits of one another. Lucien Pissarro
made this portrait of Vincent while he was sitting on a bench talking. He could talk the hind leg off a donkey, my brother!

*Émile Bernard, Iron Bridge
near Asnières, 1887. Oil on
canvas*

*Georges Seurat, Portrait of
Paul Signac, 1889-90.
Pencil drawing*

In spring Vincent hung around a lot with Paul Signac. This portrait
of him drawn in pencil was made by his friend Georges Seurat.

Henri and Vincent are both a bit pigheaded but they understand one another. Henri draws mainly in bars, theatres,
and restaurants. Just like Vincent he prefers to draw people
in different poses: sitting, reclining, standing, and dancing.
Mostly women subjects, because he likes women a lot.
The posters he makes for the theater are hanging up all over
town. I have bought a painting from him for my own collection. It is a portrait of a young woman sitting at a table,
staring dreamily into space.

Émile Bernard was nineteen years old when he met my
brother. Émile is fifteen years younger than Vincent. After
two years of lessons at the Cormon studio Émile has had
enough of it. He wants to be free to experiment with new
painting techniques. I wonder whether the two of them
were working together in the open air when they both
painted the iron bridge near Asnières. Émile's painting is
really mysterious with those black figures. He paints so
differently from my brother.

Shortly before he left for Paris, Vincent visited Georges's studio for the first time. He thinks his paintings are very good. Georges is absolutely mad about color. He reads all the books about it. He paints thousands of colored dots, one next to the other. From a distance the dots seem to move and dance in front of your eyes. All these different-colored dots melt into one another. He uses his colors straight out of the tube, sometimes mixing them first with white. This is the way he is trying to paint light. The park is popular with townspeople on Sundays, as they want to enjoy their day off. It is wonderfully cool under the trees near the water.

Vincent has used the dot technique in his paintings as well, but not like Georges Seurat, who doesn't want to leave anything to chance.

Vincent met Louis Anquetin at Cormon's studio too. They go with Émile Bernard to the attic of Siegfried Bing, a dealer they are friendly with. There you can find a complete collection of Japanese prints. Vincent and I had already bought Japanese prints at Bing's for our art collection. Louis and Émile were extremely enthusiastic about them. The Japanese use such bright colors and draw such flowing lines! I wonder if I will see the 'Japanese' influence in his paintings.

Opposite: Georges Seurat,
A Sunday Afternoon on the
Island of La Grande Jatte,
1884-1886. Oil on canvas

✒ Painting using lines or thousands of colored dots.

You will *need* thick paper, a pencil, paint, and several different brushes.

Georges Seurat used thousands of colored dots in his paintings. This technique is called the 'pointillist' style. Choose a subject to paint. For example a garden, park or plant. Take two small sheets of paper. On the first sheet you paint your subject in lines. On the second sheet you paint the same subject in dots of different colors. Stand back and look at your painting at regular intervals. Can you see what happens to the colored dots? Which painting took you longer to do?

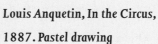

Louis Anquetin, In the Circus,
1887. Pastel drawing

29

Portrait of Père Tanguy,
1887-1888. Oil on canvas

Totally mad about Japanese prints

The paint merchant Père Tanguy is a good friend of
my brother's. He tries to sell Vincent's paintings, but
unfortunately he hasn't been successful up until now.
Even if a painting of Vincent's is not completely dry,
Père Tanguy puts it up in the middle of his shop window.

In the portrait you can see the holy mountain Fuji and
Japanese prints all around him. With his folded hands he
seems to me like a Buddhist priest.

But I never see Japanese prints in Père Tanguy's window,
so my brother must have invented them. If an artist hasn't
got any money, that's no problem for Père Tanguy. You just
pay him with a painting! But Père Tanguy buys paintings
from the artists too. His shop sometimes looks more like
an art dealer's than a paint shop. It is very near; that is why
I go in there quite often. It is always enjoyable because a
lot of people go round there to have a look. For the painting of himself, Père Tanguy is demanding an extra high
price. If you ask me, he doesn't want to sell it at all.

Vincent is absolutely mad about Japanese prints. For
him they are the best examples of how to do colorful,
bright paintings. Actually, Vincent thinks that all artists
should have a look at them. He is very busy organizing an
exhibition of the Japanese prints.

In order to get to know the prints better, he is copying
them. They are never exactly the same: he just can't resist
thinking up new additions or changing the originals.

Vincent in the South of France

All at once we were saying goodbye, it happened so quickly

February 1888

'Whatever is going on?' My entire apartment is full of Japanese prints hanging all over the walls. It seems as if my house has been converted into a cheerful Japanese world. It is just like Vincent to do something like that. But the surprise hasn't cheered me up, because all at once we were saying goodbye, it happened so quickly. Recently I have been totally preoccupied with my work and Jo. I am madly in love with her, I have just sent a letter to her in The Netherlands. I hope that she will start to have feelings for me.

Vincent will now be sitting in the train, away from the hustle and bustle of Paris. He was so totally exhausted, it had stopped him from painting. At last Vincent is going to the countryside, to Arles, right down in the South of France. We have talked about it so much. He wants to set up an artists' house there where painters can live and work. It remains to be seen whether it will be a success with all those pig-headed young men together in one studio.

Vincent believes that the light and colors are brighter in the south. He sees the south as France's Japan.

It is quiet in the house without Vincent. He has only just left but I miss him already. To console myself I am looking at one of his paintings, a beautiful pale-green landscape.

*Arles, Mount Montmajour,
where the ruin of a monastery
can be found*

A white world of snow

There is a letter lying on the doormat, hopefully good news, because I am worried about whether Vincent will be able to find a good spot. I read that Vincent has rented a room in a hotel. On the way there in the train, the white hilltops against the clear blue sky made him think of the Japanese prints.

Arles is covered in a thick layer of snow. Vincent is painting the view from the window of his hotel.
As soon as the snow starts to melt he wants to explore the surroundings. But there is still a chilly wind, which gives him goose flesh. Vincent will have to wait awhile before he can paint outside.

Blossoming Plum Tree, 1888.
Oil on canvas

The Painter on the Way to
Tarascon, 1888. Oil on canvas

Vincent on his way to paint

I think that is such a beautiful portrait of Vincent. He is on his way
to a good spot for painting. Now I have a better idea of how he goes
about it. His sun hat protects him from the bright sun. He clamps his
stretched canvas under his left arm and holds his painting materials
in his right hand while carrying an artist's easel on his back.

The colors are appearing again

The landscape around Arles is flat, and the soil is a beautiful shade of red. It is planted with grapevines, and in the distance you can glimpse the lilac hills. Vincent always writes so beautifully about everything he sees around him. On one hill there is a the ruin of a monastery. The hill itself is completely overgrown by shrubs, and there are olive trees and pine trees everywhere. I think Vincent sees a new painting in everything. He writes about the brilliant sunshine that melts the snow. He is happy that the colors are reappearing again.

The postman brought a painting of Vincent's today. To my surprise I saw that the colors were all cheerful. Vincent has written to me that he doesn't dare roll up all the paintings to send to me. The layers of paint on them are so thick that they just won't dry. He writes that he is painting only trees in blossom, and orchards, which are to form a complete series. It is blowing so hard that he has to fasten his easel to the ground with sturdy pegs. He has to be quick because the blossoms are being blown off the trees in no time at all.

Vincent has asked me once again for new tubes, even though I have just sent him a whole collection of oil paints! 'But if you can't afford it, I can always do drawings instead because that costs almost nothing,' he writes, 'as then all I need is paper and ink and a pen, which I can make myself.' Vincent hopes I can sell his paintings of trees, but people will have to like them. I must make sure that Vincent's paintings can be seen at an important exhibition in Paris.

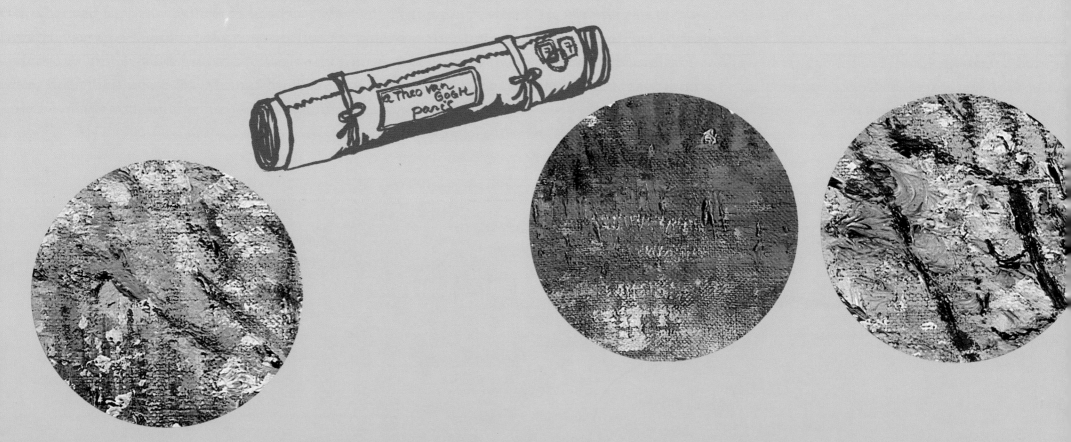

vincent
La Crau
Vue prise à Mont major

Under the scorching sun

'Every day the scorching sun appears in the sky,' Vincent writes. However, he doesn't bother much about the heat. Vincent wants to paint the people at work, but they are barely conspicuous in that panoramic landscape. He is working outside all day in the scorching sun and carries on in the evening in his studio.

Vincent has sent someone we know a few reed pens. It seems he is very impressed with reed pens. He writes that the reeds are growing everywhere along the canals, that you can break them off just like that. At home you can cut a reed to give it a good tip, and then you have a handy pen to draw with. That brother of mine never fails to amaze me. Vincent is planning on drawing a lot more with them.

There seems to be a superb view from the hill where the ruined monastery is. Despite the mistral – which just carries on blowing – and the biting mosquitoes, Vincent has continued to slog away. He first makes a sketch in pencil, after which he continues with a reed pen or a goose quill. In his studio he has drawn two people walking.

Vincent would like a bamboo frame around the drawing. Then it would look even more Japanese.

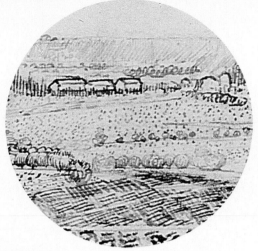

A drawing without color in dots, lines, wavy lines, and curvy lines

You will need drawing paper, pen and nib or quill-pen, black or brown ink, fountain pen, or fine felt-tip pen.

Vincent drew the landscape with endless patience. Look how precisely he has drawn it. Do a drawing of a landscape or choose a different subject, for example the view from your room. Just like Vincent, use only black or brown ink for your drawing.

Opposite: The 'La Crau' Plain Seen from Montmajour, 1888. Drawing, pencil, and black and brown ink

The sower sowing the seeds

A short while ago Vincent asked me if I could send him a print after a drawing by Millet. Millet remains his great model. He has been dreaming of doing a painting of the sower for so long, Millet's sower in color, and big!

Vincent is painting a piece of land with the earth ploughed up in violet, and in the distance the ripe corn in ocher yellow. And the setting sun colors the sky completely yellow. The field is still sparkling from the after-effects of the sunlight. The sower is sowing the seeds in the ploughed-up soil. Vincent couldn't care less about what the colors look like in reality. He has written to me that he is using extra bright colors because he knows that in time they will fade.

In the field Vincent thinks a lot about the old times, when we were young. If only I could go back with him for awhile, back to the time when we rolled around in the grass and got a stomach ache from laughing so much.

Sower with Setting Sun,
1888. Oil on canvas

Pavement Café on the Place du Forum by Night, 1888.
Oil on canvas

Painting at night

This is the first painting that Vincent made of the town of Arles. It is a pavement café. He sometimes goes for a drink there himself.

It was very clear that night, with a star-studded sky. Vincent says that he has put up his easel in the street and has just started to paint. He has often talked about his plan to make a painting of the night. The light isn't coming just from the stars but from the windows, too. There are lamps and candles burning everywhere. People sitting at the pavement café are sipping their drinks and chatting. A coach comes rattling into the street.

A house at Place Lamartine no. 2

In May Vincent rented a house. The house has four rooms, and it is painted on the outside. Because he wants to make it look good, he has asked me for extra money for the furnishings. There would appear to be a marvelous room upstairs with a view of a park. He would like to use this to put up his guests. Downstairs there are two studios, so one can be used as a kitchen.

Vincent is keen on Gauguin coming to Arles to stay as a guest in his artists' house. He has already written to him a few times to ask him to go and stay there. But Paul is making Vincent wait for an answer. Could it be that he doesn't feel like going there at all? I'll make Paul an offer, because I know he has money problems. What about if I were to buy a painting from him?

The Yellow House

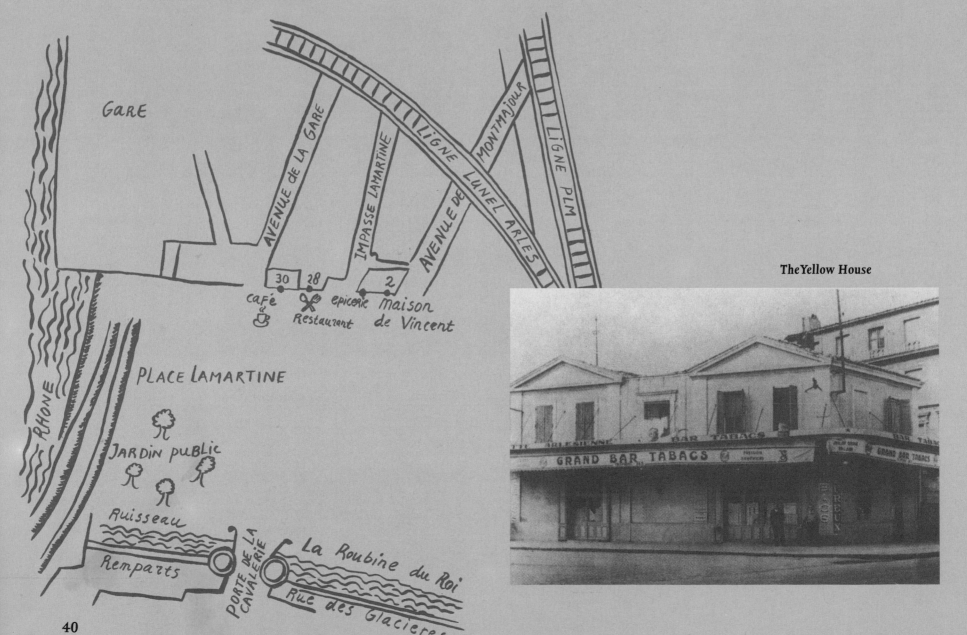

40

Portrait of Joseph Roulin,
pen with brown ink

The portrait drawing of Joseph Roulin has been drawn after a painting. Vincent is planning on doing portraits of the entire Roulin family.

L'Arlésienne: Mme Joseph-
Michel Ginoux, 1888.
Oil on canvas

Wouldn't it be great if Paul would go? I am worried about Vincent being on his own too much because he is painting the whole day long. Fortunately, he's met the postman, Roulin, who is full of stories. They spend hours together in the evenings in Café de la Gare. The proprietress of the bar, Madame Ginoux, has also become a good friend of Vincent's. She likes reading books just like Vincent does.

Paul Gauguin in Arles

Vincent is very satisfied with the furnishings in his bedroom. There are red flagstones on the floor, and the big wooden furniture gives it a restful atmosphere. He has bought a lovely warm blanket for his bed so this is a room he can really relax in.

Fortunately Paul Gauguin has written a letter to say he wants to go to Arles after all. I have made a deal with him to buy one painting of his a month. This will give me a good collection of Paul's paintings. Vincent will be so happy!

As a special surprise for Paul, Vincent wants to decorate the entire house with twelve paintings of sunflowers. He thinks that a house without paintings on the walls is not an artists' house. It's just typical of my brother to want to do something so impossible. After all, he can't carry on working day and night, can he? He already has enough canvases to fill all the walls in the house if he were to hang them up.

Twelve Sunflowers in a Vase,
1888. Oil on canvas

 Paint your own bedroom

You will need drawing paper, a pencil, thick paper,
paint, and brushes.

Before you start on the painting of your bedroom, think about what is
most important for you in the room. Choose the objects or things you
want to paint. Before you start painting, first do a few sketches in pencil.

Vincent is planning to make a painting of his bedroom. He wants to paint it in even patches of color. I am curious about how it will turn out because I have only seen a sketch.

The Bedroom, 1888.

Oil on canvas

They paint together

Vincent writes that Paul is a strange person, that he doesn't get excited about things and works very hard, also that he is creative and strong. He thinks he can learn a lot from him.

They paint the same subjects together. Vincent is amazed at how smoothly Paul paints; his brushstrokes are almost invisible. He even irons his canvases to get them smoother still. There is a great difference between Vincent and Paul. Vincent paints subjects he sees, and Paul uses his imagination. Now Vincent is also trying, just like Paul, to use his imagination. They need money for paint and strong artists' cloth made of raw jute, which is what potato sacks are made of.

They are painting each other. Paul is doing a portrait of Vincent while he is painting his favorite flowers. Vincent thinks the portrait resembles him but that he looks a bit weird. Vincent is making a portrait of Paul in a red beret.

They talk for hours on end and tell each other everything. They are both so different, and they have such varying opinions that they can't always understand one other. That often leads to rows. I hope that the two of them can continue to get along with each other. Vincent is not sure whether Paul is enjoying himself. I can well believe that Paul thinks the small town of Arles is boring, he is so adventurous and loves to travel so much. Vincent is also very scared that Paul is disappointed in him and will leave for that reason.

Vincent has made a new painting of lilac poplar tree-trunks with falling leaves. He thinks I will admire it. How well my brother knows me.

On the painting I can see a depiction of only one part of the trees. They are standing like pillars along the road. The ground around the Roman tombs is covered with a thick carpet of orange and yellow leaves; they are still whirling to the ground like snowflakes.

Vincent painted it on the rough cloth that Paul had found. I see that he has tried to paint just as smoothly as Paul.

Opposite:
Les Alycamps, Falling Leaves,
1888. Oil on canvas

Three letters to Jo

I am so happy, my dear friend Jo wants to marry me after all. At the same time I feel so sad about Vincent. I must write to Jo straightaway about what has happened.

Dear Jo,

A few days ago I received the news that Vincent has been admitted to the hospital in Arles. I ran to the station at once to catch the night train. It took ages before I reached Vincent. How pale he was when I saw him in bed. Happily he was sleeping peacefully. Vincent's premonition that Paul would leave proved to be true after all.

The doctor told me that Vincent had cut off part of his own earlobe after having had an argument with Gauguin. Vincent must have been very confused. Nobody could tell me exactly what had happened. Vincent's head was swathed in bandages. He was so weak and spoke so softly that I could barely understand him. I had to get back to Paris. Can you imagine how difficult it was to leave him behind like that?

It would be nice if you could come to Paris soon.

Love, Theo

Dear Jo,

I am working hard to find a house for us to live in together. It isn't easy to find something good. There must be enough room for Vincent's paintings. They are hanging up and lying around all over the place at the moment, even under the bed. You don't have to worry so much about Vincent anymore, as he wrote to me saying that he was getting better. He feels a lot more calm. Vincent thinks it is so awful for me that I went all the way to see him that night, but he is my brother after all, isn't he?

I am glad to say he is back in the yellow house again. His friend Roulin has cleaned the entire house and done the shopping for him. Vincent has slowly begun painting again, a still life. It is a painting of his table at which he writes all his letters. Lying on the table are his familiar belongings, which are now very important to him. There are also some onions on it too. He had read that the scent of onions was good for curing sleeplessness. Vincent will feel awful that Paul left so suddenly. It must be quiet in the yellow house.

I am very tired so I am going to put this letter into an envelope. I'll write to you again soon! With a kiss from your Theo.

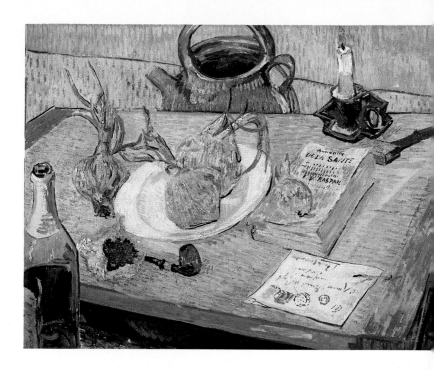

Still Life with Onions, 1889.
Oil on canvas

Sleeproom at the Hospital of
Arles, 1889. Oil on canvas

Self-portrait with Bandaged
Ear, 1889. Oil on canvas

Dear Jo,

Today I got a letter from Doctor Rey. He writes that
Vincent has been admitted to hospital again. Doctor Rey
told me that people in Arles see him as a crazy, dangerous
man. They think he should be locked up. My brother
is perhaps confused but he is certainly not mad and
wouldn't hurt a fly. Doctor Rey says that Vincent may
not go outside yet.

Dear Jo, I wish you were with me to sympathize,
your Theo.

To Saint-Rémy

It is a shame that Vincent can't be at the wedding party. It would do him good to see the whole family and his friends once again. Vincent wants to move to an old monastery in Saint-Rémy, not far from Arles. He doesn't feel well, and he still has bouts of depression. He can sit at the table for days on end with his head in his hands. He hears strange voices and noises that aren't there. Nobody can help him or reassure him. He has the feeling that he can't do anything anymore.

May 1889

The old monastery is a nursing home for people who are confused and thus are no longer able to take care of themselves. There are also people living there who will never recover. If only Vincent could have stayed in the yellow house. After Gauguin left, all his plans fell through.

Time and time again I write to him to say that he is welcome in Paris, but I think he is afraid of being a burden to us. Vincent still feels guilty about the money I send him, but I have faith in him and he gives me such superb paintings in return.

We are now living in a larger apartment. Jo is making it homey. Every Sunday morning we are busy with Vincent's paintings. They move from one wall to another as we keep hanging them in different ways.

Vincent has promised to send me all his paintings. At last I shall be able to see *The Bedroom* in color. He has asked me to destroy the canvases that I think aren't good. I could never do that!

Opposite:
Monastery Garden in
Saint-Rémy, 1889.
Oil on canvas

48

Vincent tells me that the monastery is surrounded by high fir trees. In the monastery garden, grass grows everywhere, choked with weeds. He is already making plans to go on trips again. But Vincent may not paint outside the monastery garden yet because the doctors want to find out what exactly is wrong with him first.

There are more than thirty empty rooms in the old building. Vincent may use one of the rooms as a studio. Through a barred window he can see a cornfield with walls all around it. In the early morning he can see the sunrise there. Vincent writes that the food in the monastery isn't tasty, and the place smells as musty as a cockroach-infested Parisian restaurant. He says he has never felt so calm. Nevertheless I hope he doesn't stay there too long.

Like fluttering butterflies

It is spring and Vincent is really keen to get outside and paint flowers. He is still a bit scared and prefers to stay near the monastery garden because he feels safe there. Vincent writes me that there is enough to paint in the wild garden.

The blue irises are coming out now, and they look just like fluttering butterflies. Vincent must catch the flowers in time to paint them. They can bloom so profusely but they wilt quickly too.

Sometimes he goes into a cornfield to paint there but then the head nurse must go with him.

He still thinks it's a shame that his paintings won't sell. I don't know what to say to him about it anymore. Vincent asks for more brushes and paint. That is a good sign anyway.

What else flutters, crawls, or creeps?

You will need drawing paper, fine felt-tip or drawing pens, ink, and colored pencils.

Vincent thought his irises looked like butterflies fluttering around. He has painted the irises very close by. What sort of bugs would be found creeping between the leaves of the irises or in the soil?

There must be insects flying around too. Make a drawing of the creepy-crawlies you can't see in the painting but which must be there.

Opposite: Field with Irises, 1889. Oil on canvas

51

The deafening chirping of the crickets

Vincent is feeling much better. He is going out again to paint in the fields more often. In the fields there is a deafening noise of chirping crickets. The scorched grass has changed to a beautiful gold color. The cypresses stand like Egyptian obelisks in the landscape; he thinks they are wonderful. He is surprised that nobody thought of the idea of choosing them as a subject for a painting before. Vincent paints the corn, the hills, and the clouds in wavy lines using streaks of paint. Vincent wants to make something special of it just like he did with *The Sunflowers*. For my mother and sister Wil, Vincent has made a small canvas with cypresses.

A week ago I bought a magazine at the newspaper stand. I couldn't believe my eyes—an article about Vincent! It was a very positive piece, full of compliments about his work. How proud I was! The critic Albert Aurier thinks Vincent's paintings are very good. I sent the article to Vincent straight off. I thought it would cheer him up. But quite the contrary, it made him miserable. He wrote to me 'that's how I should be but I feel so much less than that.' Vincent thinks other painters are much better.

I think my brother is too hard on himself. He is never satisfied. But his paintings have been given such powerful colors which you don't see very often. What he makes is so real. They aren't beautiful pictures but they do show his own world. In Paris I don't know a single painter who paints like my brother.

We have had a son! We are so happy with him. He cries the whole day long but that doesn't matter because he is an absolute darling. He's called Vincent Willem after my brother Vincent.

Opposite:
Cornfield with Cypresses,
1889. Oil on canvas

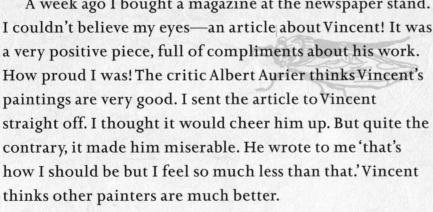

Men Digging up a Tree Stump,
1890. Oil on canvas

Vincent is working on a painting with diggers. As models for the diggers, he has asked me to send prints by Millet. Vincent has already made more paintings after Millet's prints. I have a number of canvases in my apartment. He calls them his 'memories of Brabant,' but now in the middle of a southern French landscape!

I have written to Vincent to tell him that I think they are really beautiful and that the paintings make me think of the old days when we used to play together on the farm. I packed a number of prints by Millet in Dutch newspapers and sent them off.

Vincent meets Jo and young Vincent

May 1890

Vincent arrived this morning and has seen Jo for the first time. I couldn't sleep last night for worry. I was frightened that something terrible would happen on the way. Vincent's been ill for so long, and that has weakened him. But I needn't have worried; when he stepped onto the platform, I saw a strong Vincent with a healthy outdoor complexion. We gave each other a great hug and made silly jokes.

Not long afterward we were standing next to little Vincent Willem's bed, peering down at him. I saw that Vincent, just like me, had tears in his eyes. 'You mustn't spoil him too much,' he said to Jo.

The next day

Vincent got up early today and was standing looking at his paintings with his sleeves rolled up. They are hanging all over the place. In the bedroom there's *The Blossoming Orchard*, in the dining room, *The Potato Eaters*, and above the piano, *Branches of Almond Blossom*, the Japanese painting that Vincent made specially when Vincent Willem was just born. The guest room is still full of paintings too.

We spread them out on the floor with some care and talked about them endlessly. We counted the paintings and found out that in the last year Vincent has made one hundred and forty paintings! It is so special to have my brother staying with us but at the same time so usual and familiar.

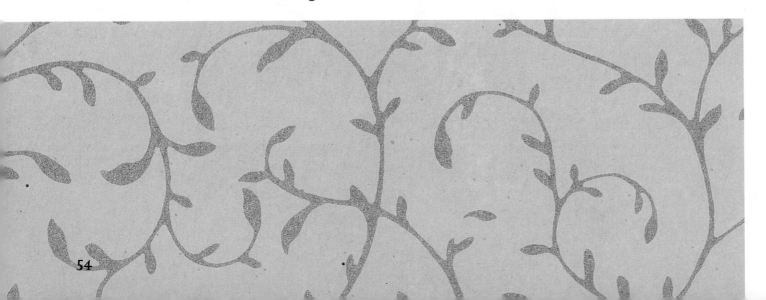

Jo and little Vincent

Theo

Vincent went to get some olives that afternoon right away. In Saint-Rémy he ate them every day, so he thought we should try them.

Lots of people come to visit. Everyone is keen on seeing Vincent. He is very gay but it is soon too busy for him. He has been alone such a lot this last year, and he isn't used to all this attention anymore. It quickly gets to be too much for him.

Vincent is moving to the village of Auvers. It is only an hour by train from Paris. Now I can go to see him more often. The village is very pretty and lies between rolling hills.

A doctor lives there. He is called Gachet, and he paints just for pleasure. He has many artist friends. I have been to Gachet's before and talked to him about Vincent. He is very friendly and I think that he'll understand my brother. Vincent's bound to like it there.

Painting in the fields of Auvers

May 1890

In Auvers, Vincent went straight round to see Doctor Gachet. They got on well from the start. Vincent was able to rent a cheap room at an inn. He thinks Auvers is beautiful; the houses have old thatched roofs and that is something that is becoming rare. Vincent wants to start painting the houses and hopes to earn a lot of money from the paintings.

Photograph of the Auberge Ravoux, the inn where Vincent was lodging

Portrait of Doctor Gachet with Foxgloves, 1890. Oil on canvas

He is planning on painting two days a week at Doctor Gachet's or on working in his garden where he grows the most superb flowers and herbs. Doctor Gachet's house is on a hill. The rooms are full of old things and there are paintings hanging up everywhere. Not much light gets inside because the window-panes are very small. Gachet paints for pleasure and is very curious to see what Vincent the artist makes.

Vincent thinks Gachet is very kind and writes to me that he could well have been an older brother of ours.

Doctor Gachet has a sad air about him. Vincent thinks that he greatly misses his dead wife. Gachet sympathizes with Vincent just as much as his sweet friend Mrs. Ginoux in Arles used to do. The portraits of Mrs. Ginoux and Doctor Gachet are very similar. The doctor is holding his careworn head in his hand. He is troubled by black moods, just like Vincent. The sprig of a medicinal herb tells you something about his profession.

Gachet has a beautiful daughter, who is called Marguerite. Vincent wants to paint her portrait. Gachet has promised to do his best to find even more interesting models for him. Vincent still prefers to paint portraits, but different from photographs. Vincent is entering into the project for all he is worth, asking himself how someone feels and what their thoughts are. He wants to paint this hidden world.

I can hear young Vincent crying. I'll go and console him right away. We must go to Auvers soon to see Vincent once again.

Church in Auvers, 1890.

Oil on canvas

The church is a purplish-blue and stands out against a deep-blue sky. The foreground is a little bit green with white and yellow flowers. The pink sunlight is shining on the sand. It is just like Vincent to make something special of an ordinary village church. It has become a moving and undulating church.

A beautiful summer's day at Vincent's

We have been invited to spend a day in Auvers at Doctor Gachet's. As our train arrived at the station Vincent was standing waiting on the platform. He had brought a bird's nest for his little nephew. 'He'll put that to pieces in no time,' I warned him. Vincent laughed. He wanted to carry our little boy himself and show him all the animals in Doctor Gachet's garden.

At the house we were warmly welcomed by Gachet. Ducks, chickens, turkeys, and peacocks were grubbing about in the grass. When the cockerel suddenly started to crow it made little Vincent cry 'That now is a cockerel crowing,' said big Vincent with a smile.

In the shadow of the large tree Marguerite laid the table. While she was doing that, Vincent showed us the flower garden. Soon afterwards the most delicious things were laid out

Village Street and Steps with Five Figures, 1890. Oil on canvas

Marguerite Gachet in the Garden, 1890. Oil on canvas

ready, fresh bread, all sorts of fruit, and carafes of fresh water. I sat next to Vincent at the table. It wasn't that long since we had seen one another, but once more we had a lot to catch up on.

After the meal we all went for a walk; it was such glorious weather. We first walked through the village, and after that went into the rolling fields. Vincent pointed out to us the places where he had been painting and where he still wanted to go and paint. I wish that day could have lasted forever. It was so peaceful and so good to be with one another.

I think Vincent is doing fine, only he looks a bit tired. He works much too hard.

 The most beautiful garden you have ever seen
You will need thick drawing paper, colored pencils, paint or watercolors, and brushes, scissors, glue, and colored paper.

Doctor Gachet's garden was superb. Imagine what your most beautiful garden would look like. You can have flowers growing in it that don't really exist, or trees full of fruit. There might be birds of paradise flying around or prehistoric animals roaming about. Or is there a fountain in the middle of it? When doing your painting make use of the different materials and techniques you have practiced earlier in this book.

The Garden at Daubigny, 1890.

Oil on canvas

Vincent hadn't been in Auvers for very long when he heard that the painter Charles-François Daubigny (1817–1878) had lived there too. He had a house and studio built there. The painter is dead but his wife still lives there. Vincent was absolutely set on making a painting of the house because he greatly admires Daubigny.

Vincent describes the colors of the painting with his sketch: 'In the foreground is a rose, and green grass. On the left a lilac shrub and a strip of plants with white leaves. On the right is a nut tree with purple leaves which juts out over the wall. The pink house has blue roof tiles. A figure in the garden is wearing a yellow hat. The air is pale green.' In my mind I can just imagine the painting. Vincent is making another painting of the garden in his studio which he is planning on giving to Daubigny's widow.

In Vincent's letter I have found a list of paints that he needs. I have noticed that Vincent is worried; he is frightened that – what with my family to support and my plans for a business of my own – there won't be enough money left to send some to him. Jo is going to write Vincent a letter right away. She wants to make it clear to him that he doesn't have to worry about money. I can tell that Vincent thinks it is really awful that he can't sell anything.

Vincent is painting a lot, but he writes that it is often an effort for him to hold his brush properly. Is he tired? He is painting large canvases of the vast fields. Vincent is absolutely mad about the landscape with the cornfields.

'They are just as vast as the sea' he says. The corn rustles and waves in the wind. He is painting a cornfield with crows and dark clouds.

I find Vincent's last letter very melancholy. Is he feeling lonely? I don't know anymore because the last time I saw him he looked so happy and was so keen on everything.

Cornfield with Crows, 1890.
Oil on canvas

I can hardly believe it

July 1890

My brother Vincent is no more. I can hardly believe it. In the bedroom I can hear Jo singing songs to little Vincent. It is Sunday today; I intend to stay indoors all day. In the dining room, surrounded by Vincent's paintings, I am constantly reminded of him.

More than a week has passed since I received the letter from Doctor Gachet. 'Vincent is seriously wounded,' he wrote me.

I traveled straight to Auvers. When I went into the dining room of the Ravoux inn, I saw Doctor Gachet sitting bent over a table. I shall never forget his worried look. Never have I been so alarmed. He told me that Vincent had shot himself in the chest with a gun. There was nothing more he could do for him. Doctor Gachet walked with me to the little bedroom upstairs.

There lay Vincent, my poor brother. I don't understand. I had bought paint for him the day before. I went and sat as close as I could to Vincent. He was very weak. I laid my head next to his on the pillow. It was just as if we were two small boys again. I didn't let him see how frightened I was that he might die. I kept telling myself that Vincent was very strong. We talked the whole night long. Very early in the morning, after the birds had just woken up, my dearest brother Vincent died.

The following morning Doctor Gachet was the first to arrive with an enormous bunch of sunflowers. Vincent would have thought they were marvelous. A little later his friends arrived. Vincent's coffin stood in the middle of the room. They had decorated all the walls with his paintings. We buried Vincent at a spot in the middle of the cornfields.

Jo is suddenly standing next to me. I didn't hear her coming. She looks beautiful. 'Don't be so sad,' she says sweetly, and she puts her soft arm around me.

Vincent died on July 29, 1890. Theo became seriously ill and died six months later on January 25, 1891. This is the spot where the two brothers are buried next to one another.

Illustrations

Unless otherwise specified, the paintings and drawings listed below are by Vincent van Gogh. The credits are provided in the order in which the works appear in the book.

Portrait photographs of Vincent van Gogh. Amsterdam, Van Gogh Museum (Vincent van Gogh Foundation)

Portrait photograph of Theo van Gogh. Amsterdam, Van Gogh Museum (Vincent van Gogh Foundation)

Photograph of Goupil's art gallery, The Hague. Amsterdam, Van Gogh Museum (Vincent van Gogh Foundation)

Photograph of Jean-François Millet, 1856. Los Angeles, The J. Paul Getty Museum

Drawing, *Woman Churning Butter*, Etten, 1881. Otterlo, Kröller-Müller Museum

Print, Jean-François Millet, *Woman Churning Butter*, 1855-56. Los Angeles, The J. Paul Getty Museum

Painting, Jean-François Millet, *Man with a Hoe*, 1860-62. Los Angeles, The J. Paul Getty Museum

Drawing, *Farmer Leaning on a Spade*, 1881. Otterlo, Kröller-Müller Museum

Drawing, *Rectory Garden with Lean-To*, 1881 Otterlo, Kröller-Müller Museum

Drawing, *Carpenter's Shed and Yard*, 1882. Otterlo, Kröller-Müller Museum

Drawing, *Weaver*, 1884. Amsterdam, Van Gogh Museum (Vincent van Gogh Foundation)

Painting, *The Potato Eaters*, 1885. Amsterdam, Van Gogh Museum (Vincent van Gogh Foundation)

Photograph, *Building of the Eiffel Tower*, 1888. Los Angeles, The J. Paul Getty Museum

Painting, *Self-Portrait Wearing a Gray Felt Hat*, 1888. Amsterdam, Van Gogh Museum (Vincent van Gogh Foundation)

Painting, *Self-Portrait*, 1887. Chicago, Art Institute of Chicago

Painting, *Bridges over the Seine near Asnières*, 1887. New York, Gagosian Gallery

Photograph, *Vincent with Bernard on the Bank of the Seine*, 1886. Amsterdam, Van Gogh Museum (Vincent van Gogh Foundation)

Painting, *Bowl with Sunflowers, Roses and Other Flowers*, 1886. Mannheim, Stadtische Kunsthalle

Painting, *Two Cut Sunflowers*, 1887. Bern, Kunstmuseum

Drawing, Lucien Pissarro, *Vincent in Conversation*, 1887. Oxford, Ashmolean Museum

Photograph, *Henri de Toulouse-Lautrec in His Studio*. Albi, Musée Toulouse de Lautrec

Drawing, Georges Seurat, *Portrait of Paul Signac*, 1889-90. St. Louis, The St. Louis Art Museum

Painting, Émile Bernard, *Iron Bridge near Asnières*, 1887. New York, The Museum of Modern Art

Painting, Georges Seurat, *A Sunday Afternoon on the Island of La Grande Jatte*, 1884-86. Chicago, The Art Institute of Chicago

Painting, Louis Anquetin, *In the Circus*. New York, Museum of Modern Art

Painting, *Portrait of Père Tanguy*, 1887-88. Paris, Musée Rodin

Photograph, Tralbout, *Mount Montmajour in Arles*. Amsterdam, Van Gogh Museum (Vincent van Gogh Foundation)

Painting, *Blossoming Plum-Tree*, 1888. Edinburgh, National Gallery of Scotland

Painting, *The Painter on the Way to Tarascon*, 1888. Burned in World War II

Drawing, *The 'La Crau' Plain, Seen from Montmajour*, 1888. Amsterdam, Van Gogh Museum (Vincent van Gogh Foundation)

Painting, *Sower with Setting Sun*, 1888. Otterlo, Kröller-Müller Museum

Painting, *Pavement Café at the Place du Forum by Night*, 1888. Otterlo, Kröller-Müller Museum

Drawing, *Portrait of Joseph Roulin*, 1888. Los Angeles, The J. Paul Getty Museum

Painting, *L'Arlésienne, Mme Ginoux with Books*, 1888. New York, The Metropolitan Museum of Art

Painting, *Twelve Sunflowers in a Vase*, Munich, Bayerische Staatgemaldesammlungen, Neue Pinakothek

Painting, *The Bedroom*, 1888. Amsterdam, Van Gogh Museum (Vincent van Gogh Foundation)

Painting, *Les Alycamps, Falling Leaves*, Otterlo, Kröller-Müller Museum

Painting, *Self-Portrait with Bandaged Ear*, 1889

Painting, *Still-life with Onions*, 1889. Otterlo, Kröller-Müller Museum

Painting, *Sleeproom at the Hospital of Arles*, 1889. Winterthur, Oskar Reinhart Collection

Painting, *Monastery Garden in Saint-Rémy*, Otterlo, Kröller-Müller Museum

Painting, *Irises*, 1889. Los Angeles, The J. Paul Getty Museum

Painting, *Men Digging Up a Tree Stump*, 1890. Detroit, The Detroit Institute of Arts

Painting, *Cornfield with Cypresses*, 1889. London, National Gallery

Photograph of Jo and Vincent Willem. Amsterdam, Van Gogh Museum (Vincent van Gogh Foundation)

Photograph of Theo van Gogh. Amsterdam, Van Gogh Museum (Vincent van Gogh Foundation)

Painting, *Portrait of Doctor Gachet with Foxgloves*, 1890. Paris, Musée d'Orsay

Painting, *Church in Auvers*, 1890. Paris, Musée d'Orsay

Painting, *Village Street and Steps with Five Figures*, 1890. St. Louis, The St. Louis Art Museum

Painting, *Marguerite Gachet in the Garden*, 1890. Paris, Musée d'Orsay

Painting, *The Garden at Daubigny*, 1890. Hiroshima, Hiroshima Museum of Art

Painting, *Cornfield with Crows*, 1890. Amsterdam, Van Gogh Museum (Vincent van Gogh Foundation)

Photograph, Ed van der Elsken, *Auvers sur Oise*, 1952. Rotterdam, Netherlands Photographic Archives

Bibliography

The Letters of Vincent van Gogh, publisher Sdu, 1990

Van Gogh's Diary, Jan Hulsker, publisher Meulenhoff/Landshoff

Vincent van Gogh, Paintings, Evert van Uitert, Louis van Tilborgh, and Sjraar van Heugten, publisher Arnoldo Mondadori Arte en de Luca Edizione d'arte, 1990

Vincent van Gogh, Paintings, Johannes van der Wolk, Ronald Pickvance, E. B. F. Pey, publisher Arnoldo Mondadori Arte en de Luca Edizione d'arte, 1990

Vincent van Gogh, Drawings, 1880-1883, Sjraar van Heugten, Van Gogh Museum, Amsterdam; Bussum, V+K publishing/Inmerc, 1996

Vincent van Gogh, Drawings, 1883-1885, Sjraar van Heugten, Van Gogh Museum, Amsterdam; Blaricum, V+K publishing/Immerc. 1997

Vincent van Gogh, Drawings, 1885-1888, Marije Vellekoop, Sjraar van Heugten, Van Gogh Museum, Amsterdam; Blaricum, V+K publishing, 2001

Vincent van Gogh, Paintings, 1881-1885, Louis van Tilborgh, Marije Vellekoop, Van Gogh Museum Amsterdam; Blaricum, V+K Publishing/Inmerc, 1999

Brief Happiness, the Correspondence of Theo van Gogh and Jo Bonger, Han van Crimpen, Leo Jansen, and Jan Robert, publisher Waanders, Zwolle, 1988

Van Gogh and Millet, Ronald de Leeuw, Louis van Tilborgh, Sjraar van Heugten, publisher Waanders, Zwolle 1988

Vincent van Gogh and the Painters of the Petit Boulevard, Elizabeth C. Childs, John House, Richard Thomson, St. Louis Art Museum in association with Rizzoli International Publications Inc., 2001

The World of Vincent van Gogh, Portraits and Self-portraits, Ronald Dorn, George S. Keyes, Joseph Rishel, Katerine Sachs et al., publisher Waanders, Zwolle, 2000

Theo van Gogh, Chris Stolwijk, Richard Thomson, Sjraar van Heugten, Van Gogh Museum, Amsterdam, publisher Waanders, Zwolle, 1999